Sick Notes

Sammy Hutton

BookLeaf Publishing

Presentation by *BookLeaf Publishing*

Web: www.bookleafpub.com

E-mail: info@bookleafpub.com

ISBN: 978-93-95784-48-1

First edition 2022

Keep Still

Keep still.
The morning lies shapelessly in the future.
Imagine that time has stretched itself in front of
you.
Notice sleep is still heavy on your skin, in your
lungs.
Close your eyes, this room holds no mystery for
you;
enduring walls, enduring air.
Focus on your finger tips; rich with thick cotton
stitches.
Smooth your hands over a crisp landscape that
rests faintly
on your skin, white sheets like paper snow.
Do not stir.
Do not stir an inch, there is nothing out there, I
swear.
You can indulge this dilated time a little longer.
Relax your face and imagine that your skin sits
as lightly on it
as the sheets lay across your body, as
autonomous too.
The pillow case creases are still there,
you can feel them if you try,

woven into the surface like a ghost from a cotton
lullaby.
Now, let those hungry hands comb in fistfuls of
heavy cotton,
bring them up toward your face,
let the map of creases reunite with your skin,
white paper doll, fragile thing.
Open your mouth and let the weight seep in,
swallowing down behind feathery teeth.
Allow veracious lungs to inhale starched sheets,
white pleats.
Don't move and very soon you'll sleep.
The day can wait for you.

Winter Caw

The summer crows arrive
Too early, and ask me what have I done?
In eastern sun
Here come the tears
As I long for a winter caw

The crows bring promises of
More time and again,
Endure! Endure! They caw
And I cry at nothing.
Bring me winter mornings,
Soaked black with night
Where I can swallow the day whole
like some desperate pill.

In winter
I can build a fire, I can throw a punch!
Sticky shadows chisel edges off buildings
And I can walk in the mornings again.
Now I am mocking crows
Look what I have done! And
The tears never come.

Melancholia

Please don't ask me to describe this colour to
you.
The words will too quickly become unlinked,
Drenched in metaphor,
Tangential.
Can't you see that in trying to describe it,
It will change?
It's elusive nature will move to the edge of my
eye
And I will dizzy myself chasing it.

I know you want to understand
But what this colour does to me cannot be
transferred.
If you want to discuss it, we must also delve into
Transparency. Viscosity. Liminality of time.
The sea is not a shade of blue,
And I too am not seeing with such singularity.

I don't know what to tell you,
I know we both see how awful it makes me
But what escape is there from this
Coating. This wash.
This sticky suffocating shade of
What I am sick with.

What You Never Knew

What you never knew was that
When the beasts became too loud
There was nothing I could do
But offer up myself

I wrapped you in worn cotton,
Draped it over the bunk bed
Torch light beamed through
Dotted sheets
And I said you would be safe.

What you never knew was that
When the beasts came too close,
There was nothing I could do
But run from where you were

I left you encased in linen
Turning loose pine spindles round and round
Like I taught you
Tightening invisible locks
Protecting you.

What you never knew was that
When the beasts finally rested
There was nothing I could do
But lift you from the bottom bunk

And begin the day again.

Dilated Time

I believe in parallel universes,
in decisions made and not made, chances taken
and encounters missed.
I believe in haunting pasts and unreachable
futures for most of us.
I believe in better things and worse and that pain
can be relative.
I believe that time can dilate and moments
expand in front of us
Only to return when we fear them most.

Wintering Love

There is an impossibility of time circling you
and I
Where futile recurrence has us bound.
Each time finding you there among the
bookshelves,
Our love wintering.

Sewn together in lifetimes before,
Silver string, a knot pulled tight.
We know how it goes. Old love and fear
That this is the last time we say
Let's begin again.

The Carpenter's Daughter

She remembers his
Splitery joints, too rushed
Get it done.
Hands of calloused tremor
As he showed her how
To measure the lengths, to measure the space.

When she is alone she thinks
Did he ever make the wood sing?
As she polishes the grain
Making luminous lines,
A swirl, a burl
Shimmering gleam.
This is how the wood sings.

They sit on this articulated
Hinge in time. Where one historic plane
Folds flat onto the now
Each time she feels along the grain
Assessing the knots.

Pain

It will feel like hot steel
Dilating time and
High tides cold hands
Invisibly gripping insides.
Desperate jolting, finger pulsing,
Explosion
Of a cracked tooth.

Insomnia

Welcome to the
time
Where nothing
blooms

There is no golden
ray
No warm sun
To soothe

You are alone
in this
Liminal space in
time

There is no list of
to do
No watching
glare

Only you and this
sacred time
Where nothing
blooms

The Haven

It's hard to make a hospital
Look like a home
When everything is
some sickly shade of blue.

Reclining chairs, separated by curtains
And no beds.
You can have your phone,
but you have nothing to say.

A door is unlocked to the toilet
And inside is almost nothing.
No toilet seat, no cords, no mirror.
You have the urge to see your face.

They come at midnight and
It's time to tell the truth
About the Voice
And how it knows more than you do.

You recline in the chair and
Cover yourself in a sheet.
You watch tv
And somehow you sleep.

The Sound of Smoke

I can't say if the smoke creature has a name.
He is too elusive to inhabit one I expect.
Lungs and throat and mouth and mind, but not a
name.
Not even time, really, seems to contain him.
Shifting from one sharp instant into a clouded
year.
I feel its voice. Not guttural but lower in the
throat.
Like inhaled smoke.

I can't say how long I have known the smoke
creature
Or how we are bound. It's not something you
can ask.
I can't even tell you when he is here or in fact if
he leaves.
He seems to belong to that realm of imagery that
you can't look directly at.
And you know that if you start to chase it,
the more slippery it becomes.
Like a name on the tip of your tongue.

We have existed in this way. With countless
unknowables in his smoke.

When will I know that I've done what I am
supposed to have done?
He feeds me futures and dilates time
Let's me know all the ways that I am wrong.
He is doing his work, singing his song.
And he says that when my end comes
I will leave nothing when I'm gone.

Fatigue

It will feel like being buried
Under windswept weight
Invisible iron plates
Heavy with heat.

It will feel like gaining mass
With each inhale
Into a body that cannot connect
Legs object.

Welcome to stationary, welcome
To static. Where the sun
Watches you cry
Hot with anger, internal fervour.

It will feel like an impossible
And bitter wade
With no poison, with no pill,
Nothing tangible to explain.

Submitting to it you will wish
It were pain,
Parallel with the sky
Enduring limbs remain.

Try

Bring them your gifts
In hands too small
With grit, with grit
Fickle bird
In a tree too big

YES

I want all the trees to witness me
Fervent, and feeling what a body feels like
When it feels good.
I want this forest hot and uninterrupted
And I want it to collide with me.
I have itchy naked skin for a
Glimmer of all that isn't
Pain.
I want to be miraculous!
I want to bite down on fallen leaves in the hopes
That it changes me,
Shifts my skin to a veil less thin.
I want the branches to collapse down
All around me with verve
And feel what a yes feels like.
The cool air won't be welcome
Against my body, impatient with
Too little hope.
I want to be luminous!
So let the blackbirds sit in a ring around me and
Converge with all unresponsive nerves.
Let the wind be breath on my breath and
Fold my body like paper.
I want to strike a match
And as the fire takes us all
I want to shout YES

Entanglement

I am a stationary
Diaphanous being.
I observe each room from a threshold
Scanning it carefully
Observing each object as it occupies its place
Each surface interacts invisibly with all that
surrounds it.
Thousands of interconnections that I can
Only catch glimpses of.

And maybe if
I were a ghost fully
I could reach into those worlds and admire the
gleaming strands
Of all impossible and accidental connections
That hold this room together.
And if I let my eyes drift cloudily unfocused
I swear I can see everything dancing silently
around me
In glinting entanglement.

The Pool

I break water tension with
Spider legged finger tips
tapping ripple patterns
Rhythmic chlorine drips
Holding in my breath
Where melody exists
Submerge submerge

Orange Sun

How many times
This sunset
Have I never seen?
Where others have fallen sooner,
It's in this reality that I have persevered
To now.

What if this is the furthest
Any of us has reached?
This age, the oldest, every minute passed.
This sunset never seen
I think

To all of you my body too holds the marks
but know that I am here
to witness a changing sky over high tide and you
Are all I hold in my heart.

One of us made it, to stand tall
In front of this orange sun.

Relief

It will feel like a wave
That moves downwards instead of
Away.
Invisible circles traced on skin,
Backwards bending crack, shoulder shiver snap.
A nervous whirl
from opiate satin wraps.